Just Another Jack

The Private Lives of Nursery Rhymes

poems by

Michele Herman

Finishing Line Press
Georgetown, Kentucky

Just Another Jack

The Private Lives of Nursery Rhymes

Copyright © 2022 by Michele Herman
ISBN 978-1-64662-744-8 First Edition
All rights reserved under International and Pan-American Copyright Conventions. No part of this book may be reproduced in any manner whatsoever without written permission from the publisher, except in the case of brief quotations embodied in critical articles and reviews.

ACKNOWLEDGMENTS

"Proper Pairs" appeared in *Literary Mama*'s September 2017 issue online. "The Oldest Child's Lament" appears in my chapbook *Victory Boulevard*, published by Finishing Line Press in 2018.

With special thanks to Kathie Klein, for once again getting the picture in my head onto the cover so perfectly.

Publisher: Leah Huete de Maines
Editor: Christen Kincaid
Cover Art and Design: © Kathie Klein, 2021
Author Photo: Helane Blumfield

Order online: www.finishinglinepress.com
              also available on amazon.com

Author inquiries and mail orders:
Finishing Line Press
PO Box 1626
Georgetown, Kentucky 40324
USA

Table of Contents

Proper Pairs 1

To Have and to Hold 4

Lambkins 6

To the Pieman 10

The Oldest Child's Lament 14

Old Soul 16

Beside Her 21

Just Another Jack 26

*to John's mother, Matilda, Bo, Margueretta, Simon,
Maude, Hugh and Jack,
and to everyone in our world going through hard times*

*and to my beloved memoir students,
who know the power of persona*

Proper Pairs

I sent him off to school
each day with everything
in proper pairs,
but he came back
home with naught
but one. How does a fellow
lose a stocking, son? I'd ask.
How does he fail to see
he's short a shoe? Then the smell
of smoke upon his homespun
pants, the staying out all night.

And now the boy won't wash,
won't sweep the hay that scatters
from his bed. Like hogs
he'll never look me in the eye
despite my making him a pile
of sausages and cakes each morn.
Forgets to feed the horse, forgets
to milk the cow, disdains to go
to school and lies about it
to my face but always has a smart
excuse. If he would study
what a barrister he'd make.

My John he's still asleep
far past the rooster's crow. I tiptoe
to his corner of the room and watch
him dream, for dream he does. He twitches,
groans and even whistles in his sleep,
more active than he is awake
by far. Awake he's got the sleepy
eye but slumbering I see he's wise
and full of plans. Perhaps right now
he's digging flawless wells. Perhaps
he's dreaming schemes to get us

out of debt. But now I see he's got
his good shirt on, the fool—

he's wrinkled it and made it smell
of boy. He knows it took me weeks
to sew, he knows my thumb joints
cause me pain, he knows my eyesight's
not so strong past dusk, the only time
I have to stitch. I want to slap him silly
and I almost do. I have to cross my arms
behind my back to stop myself.

It's only later that I feel
the pain and see I've used
such force to keep myself
in check I've bruised my arms,
I've purple marks on both of them.
Not that I think he'd notice
but I wear my sweater all day long
despite the heat.

You see, I looked and looked and tried
to find my silly chubby lad,
but all I saw was hardened jaw
that's stubble-strewn, and packs
of muscle everywhere.

I finally laid a hand quite gently
on his arm the way I used to do.
He blinked until my face
came into view. Call me
by that baby name, he said,
I swear I'll…
I bit my tongue until it bled,
but still the ancient words
escaped all slicked with red:

you'll always be my babe,
my precious one,
my deedle dumpling son.

To Have and to Hold

I need, need, need the fatty cuts, the bacon fringe that crackles in the pan and on my tongue. I need the cream that quilts the milk. I slurp it up before I've hardly left the cow. And Jack? Lord love the bag of bones but long's I live I'll never understand what keeps the man alive. A man what's made of gristle, grit and muscle wrapped inside a package of the thinnest, toughest skin. He'd make a cabbage last all week, if boiled into a runny soup or pickled so it'd strip the wagon's paint, the skin right off your palm.

A perfect match, they say we are, a waste-not-want-not marriage vow. Another harvest, another loss, another tiny stone out back. Who knows why? It's true I couldn't tell when I was ripe with child because I'm pretty ripe without. My stomach's always big yet I am never full, but Jack—you put a carrot on his plate beside the whitest scrap of meat and soon he's backing up and saying how he cannot eat another bite, his chewing apparatus tired out, he's going out to have himself a smoke. He'd breathe the fumes of food much sooner than he'd chew.

Hey Jack, I say, a man can't live on gaseous states alone. Come stay and have a morsel of the pudding what I made of butter toffee with molasses on the top. Come lick a smidgeon off me little finger, it will do you good, you know. A man like you who works so hard the whole week long should send some sweetness down inside himself. I'm sorry 'Til, he shakes his head (Matilda is me proper name but he ain't one for flourishes). It ain't as though he means me harm, ain't as though he's saying no for reasons of defiance (though he does defy). It's just there's something wrong inside his gut, a different something than whatever's wrong in mine. Oh I wish we had a proper doc nearby. If only we could probe in there and fix the leak or mend the clog, then maybe we could fatten him a bit and take a bit off me and make it stick to him. I love that man, I do, as decent as they come though like I said, he's taciturn at best, not like my kin O'Malleys with our ever-open maws.

And now I feel the tug again; I wonder if a moon or two has passed since last I bled. I couldn't say, what with the harvest come around again, the 'taters being all we see and smell and touch and dream at night. Sure enough, me dugs feel raw and all swelled up like giant 'taters resting heavy on me tum, a tum that sometimes makes three rolls and sometimes hardens into one that juts. I smell the sweat that never leaves my undersides, of tits on tum, of chins on neck, so many folds and overhangs. I used to solve the chafing in between my legs with flour but to tell the truth it's getting much too hard to walk much farther than the yard. I'm growing kitchen-bound, which fuels me hunger even more. And now I fear I'll retch like him. My heart it seems to work too hard; it pounds some kind of warning message all day long. All I want's to fold me Jack, so cold, inside of me and wrap him 'round and tuck him in me fatty droops of tits and arms and thighs. If I just had the strength sometimes I think I could walk around with him embedded inside me, my only baby Sprat. Let him suckle up my milk I've plenty here to give.

Lambkins

If we Welsh have genius
it's for stiles. We live
in houses like our neighbors'
to the west and to the east,
but every stile's its own
design. To thwart
the cloven hoof—
that's what we do
the best. There's some
that like the jaws
of death they batten
down from either side,
and some use rollers
on the ground that scare me
ewes no end. Others still
work on a principle of wheels
that turn inside of other
wheels so that even I,
a lass been born and bred
on native soil, still fear to enter
them. If packs of wolves
appeared, saliva dripping
from their swinging tongues,
me woolly girls would let themselves
be supper 'fore they'd put a hoof
inside a stile. So what I mean to say's
my sheep cannot have gotten
far. (And I thank the Lord this isle
be free of wolves, for now
I've scared meself just thinking
on those narrow jaws so jammed with fangs.)

The April sun it was a'shining
on the heather early morn
and I was shining too
for the snowdrops and forsythia

had opened up their buds at dawn and Will
the dairy boy with the lovely
baritone was singing in the stall
to the tune of squirts of milk
upon the sides of pails of tin,
a jolly tune it were. The heather
on the hillside made a haze of green
and pink beyond me attic window
so I grabbed me petticoats and frock
and bonnet strings and a bit of grub
and skipped outside to meet the morn
and tend me flock. And out we went
a'roaming on the rolling
hills that have no end, it seems,
though sure they must give way
eventually to burghs or sea. The sheep
they crave their breakfast grass,
and me I've got a wedge of bread
with butter freshly churned on top
and bottom half. I've got a skin
that's filled with cider meant to soften
up the loaf. I count me sheep from one to eight:
here's Mollie Mae, here's Tinka, Tea and Bron
and Isabelle and farther out me stragglers—
the black sheep Ora-Faye and half-black
Muddy Sue and last our most-beloved
grandmama, Queen Anne.

I smile because they're so predictable,
if only tots in school would answer to the roll
as readily as they. We've far to walk
but I don't mind, the day's so fresh and I've nowhere
I have to be 'til mother yells at noon to help her
with the meal and chores. We reach our favorite spot
between two hills where water runs a path as winding

as me crook and makes a tiny tinkling noise. And here
I set me down to eat and dream of dancing
at week's end, perhaps a trot with Will. The girls
are baa-ing as they do, 'tis always Muddy Sue
who makes the first announcement of the day,
and soon the gossip makes the rounds. I feel protected
in this spot, as if I'm just a babe surrounded by
me mother's dugs. And soon I feel the sun
upon me face and arms, as if it's saying, take
a snooze, that's what such morns are for.

'Tis all me fault. I stray not bodily but in
me thoughts. I put meself a'fore me girls,
a thing I never dared before. At first I think on Pa,
who comes alive inside me memory,
a handsome, taut-skinned charmer, he.
And soon me Pa he changes shape and voice
to re-emerge as Will. I get to seeping moisture
where it's never seeped before. I see his light-brown
hair a'flapping in his daddy's cart. I get to thinking
thoughts a young girl oughtn't think. And think I do
for quite a while while lying 'tween these hills and only half
a'hearing idle baa's. Before I know the sun upon me throat
and cheeks it soothes me to a drowse and in my dream
I leap upon the dairy cart as if I had four cloven hooves,
and as if I had a milk cow's hangin' tongue I swipe it right
across the chest of Will, for it were warm enough
for him to open up a button of his homespun shirt. His chest
so smooth and soft and warm I go to take another lick
but a ringing gong it stops me dead. I wake up
from me dream and, my, I have a start.

The world beyond me sleepy lids has changed.
For now it's gray and cold and like to pour,
and sheepless, no! I roust meself and shake me sleep
away and turn me head in all directions

but I find no sheep. I call sweet Mollie Mae and Tinka,
Tea and Bron, Isabelle and Ora-Fae and Muddy Sue
and blessed Annie, come back me dears, stop kidding me
(for sheep I like to think can joke as well
as anyone). I start to run and soon I feel me pocket
and I know I've left me cider skin behind
but now I've run so far I've lost the wee small brook
as thoroughly as me sheep.

I'm on a hill that ain't familiar, heather-less but thick
with thorn and bee. Beyond it this way is another hill
and that way three small crags. I open up me mouth
to scream for sheep, but oh, me mouth is dry. I call and call
me sheepy roll. Though cold I sweat inside. I climb
this mound, I run back down to climb the craggy spot.
I cannot fathom how me girls have got so far so fast.
I cannot help but feel betrayed, and all alone
with clouds so thick I cannot find the sun to tell me
which way's east and which is west.

I call the roll, me roll calls back in echoes
off the hills. I feel the hills are swelling like to join
and squeeze me in between. The sun it pokes between
two clouds. I see it's way past noon, poor Ma at home
without no extra hands, a'worrying herself. I must get home.
I weigh me humanness against me charges' sheepiness
and don't feel sure which one of us comes out ahead.

But here is what I choose: to go on
home without me dears and trust
they'll find their way. And that,
I should be pleased to say, is just what comes
to pass, complete with wagging tails. But I
cannot help but feel I've wandered right
into a stile of sorts meself,
and cannot get back out.

To the Pieman

I ain't simple, Simon said, it's just me ears
don't hear, which gives me voice a terr'ble
task in forming well-made sounds. It's true
I wear a sack with holes for sleeves, me soles
are leather-hard—me skin, that is,
which learned to play the role
of shoes. Me parents left
me by the road and fled to who
knows where because they could not
keep a child as empty-brained as me.
But I ain't a fool, I ain't a joke, me brain
is working fine. I understand, I do,
that pie costs coins, that piemen
must be paid. But tell me, sir,
how I'm to earn my pence for food
when all the town just shakes
its head whene'er they see me face. I'm
neither dumb nor feelingless. My Ma
she didn't want to leave, I read it
in her eyes, but Pa he took her
by the arms and turned her 'round
and spoke some words that even I
could hear were meant to soothe
but bit like pox. And off they went
upon a donkey cart. They left me
with a bite to eat wrapped up
in paper, waxed. It had an oily
sheen and I were starved—they
had me number, true. And while
I pulled the paper loose and found
the pie inside, the cart kicked
dust and fled. A slice of cherry pie,
it were, a'oozin' thick and red,
its crust a'flakin' golden brown
and heavy in me hand. I looked

ahead along the lane not knowing yet
their scheme and I sat meself beneath
an oak in shelter from the morning
sun and spread the paper out. I'd never
had a treat before of such a magnitude.
Me heart it oozed with pride
and pleasure as I set to wait until
the cart came back in view so's I
could thank them properly (as proper
as a boy can do who can't form
words). The pie it sat in front of me.
I shooed the flies all morn. The sun
it moved and moved and moved
some more, the traffic in the lane it grew.
Me stomach, spared the trouble in me tongue,
it grew more loud and clear. So hollow
I began to feel inside as night began
to fall. Me pie it waited bleeding
so it stained me fingers red. And all I would
allow meself was the licking of me hands.
I told meself to make it last—who knew
when next I'd have the chance
to eat? Some lads approached with nothing
on their minds but teasing me,
their after-chore reward. And so I saw
no other choice. I scarfed the pie.
It filled me mouth so sweet
and unctuous, tart and butter-soft.
I cried and cried, so fine it were.
I cried because it was too much
and I felt sick and feared it might
heave up. The lads were coming
fast. I chewed and chewed
and coughed because me system

had no clue what it should do with all
this sudden food. Slow down, it cried
inside of me. But I kept swallowing.
Me teeth had never known such syrup
nor such dough, for all they knew
was gruel and broth and mutton stew.
They wanted more but ached and tore.
The lads they found me mouth stuffed
full, fingers slick with wondrous goo.
They smelled the sweetness on me breath
and how it made them seethe, for they
were just as poor as me, except in family.
So while the crust was gullet bound,
they found they couldn't tolerate
the sight of me—that is, much more
than usual. The biggest lad, a bully boy
named Tom, approached me with a smile,
and uttered words to this effect:
"You smell of pie, you'd better share
with us or there'll be hell to pay."
I showed me empty, sticky hands. He turned
to face the other lads as if to leave and then
his fist came at me pistol-quick and punched me
in the pie-packed gut and up it came,
but sour now, and like the fountain
in the square it arced out of me mouth
and poured in lumps on Tom.

So Mister pieman, yes I know you've mouths
to feed at home and yes I know that pie don't grow
on trees as pluckable as plums. I know it's hard
to roll a dough and cook the fruit and yes I know
that cherries come with stones that take a lot of space
inside and yes I know that ovens eat up wood.
But it's Saturday, the crowds are heading fair-ward.
If I could hear I'd know the tinkle of the coins

that bounce inside their purses. Surely you can spare a morsel for a hungry lad.

The Oldest Child's Lament

My only stab at happiness lies with the happiness
of them if no ones crying no limbs cracked and no one
pouts if Ma is trying to do right by us today at least
Ill take it and Ill say thank God for what youve given us
and if the larder has a little fat the breadbox has a half
a loaf Ill somehow make it spread to feed the kids before
I send us off to bed Im bleeding now but not from outside
or from blows by her the lads in town they smell me and
they come around Id like to go off with the lads who live
in proper lanes not plunked like us upon a field with no
address our house it smells of unwashed feet I have no
coins for bootblack to repair the wornout roof our several
fathers live in town at least we think they do she named
us well but then ran out of juice thats how she operates
Priscilla Ogden Manuel Rasputie Darla Mug and me Im
Margueretta but they call me Et which makes us laugh
cause often I aint et a crumb I try to keep us clean
I try to keep the cistern lid on tight I try to make them ruly
but without the Pas its tough I try to get the smaller ones
to school so they can teach me sums and letters I can write
a bit but dont know how to spell I can add two numbers
only if theyre small Im running out of coins and wares to sell
to keep our bellies fed our Ma is nowhere to be found
off doing who knows what I rouse the crusty smelly kids who kick
me half the time because their sleep is poor its hard to breathe
in here I open up the lace and roll the tongue up high I wish
I had some help I sweep the insole clean or cleanish anyway
and damn that tongue that rolls right back we made a porch
last year the boys and me we cut a tree and hacked it up
and Mug still has that scar above his eye each night I pray
to God with thanks he spared that eye which spared me too
I couldnt bear it if Id made him blind I dont know how I could
go on I went to town to beg the butcher for some scraps
a darkhaired boy I see in town sometimes he eyed me back
when I eyed him I ducked inside a shop to catch my breath

and watch him pass and glance my way I didnt even check
which shop it was until a female voice said not again
dear Et I gathered back my wits and saw it was
the undertakers house and she remembered Tumbeline and
Timberline the twins we tried so hard to save who perished
on day three oh no I said were all alive then added leastways
now I ask you what would make a person talk like that Ill tell
you what I hate it when someone feels bad because of me so
I was killing off my kin to give the undertaker's wife some hope
for work and here Im trying not to let the boy know how
I live and marching to a place that stinks of death oh what a dope
I think and slink on home to ready up some grub and hope
that maybe Cillas woken up more grown and ready to come help
without me begging first but Cillas staring at herself as usual
in the only window pane weve got and meantime Ogdens
punching Darla in the gut and Darlas going off to cry inside
the outhouse where I told her not to go with nothing on her feet
theres worms out there that want to get in us and once
theyre in they never leave so I breathe real slow and put my hands
on Cillas arms and whisper in her ear my Cilla dear I need
your help go try to scrounge some crusts go heat the broth
and put it in the little gourds to make it seem like more
then things get quiet under Mug which always means
theres something wrong I hoped for time to practice
with my sums I know that six and six adds up to twelve I overheard
the schoolmarm say I try to walk beside the school on scorching days
when windows all are open and I learn a bit that way and try to bring
it home but the learning sloshes in my brain like buckets overfilled
and by the time Im to the door Ive lost the bulk of it oh Ma come home
and rescue me and meantime I will save the kids Ill fold them
in my old blue skirt I found another tooth of Mas I picked it up
and saw the wrinkles running through that yellow bone the second one
this month I hid it from the kids oh Ma come back come back
in body be our Ma in mind and bring a Pa or two I beg of you
until you do Im holding down the shoe just like you asked me to.

Old Soul

He forgot the war he had declared
upon the kingdom to the east.
He forgot about the skirmish
he'd provoked because he never
liked the duke of hoosiwhats.
My pipe! my bowl! he called,
and when his valet brought them in,
he tried to smoke the bowl and put the
wrong end of the pipe into his mouth,
and when his fiddler third set down
his instrument to save his ruler's
life, the fiddler for reward received
a visage full of ash and royal phlegm.

But merry was the king, even while
quite ruddy in the face with neck
veins pumping visibly.

His wife, old Maude, came marching
in and shooed away the fiddler third.
She turned to face her mate of many
moons. "Now what fresh
mischief have you hawked, my love?"
and used her thumb to wipe saliva
from his cheek, whereupon she turned
to face the fiddlers, asking "Have you got
a buoyant tune to lighten up these moony
castle halls—mazurka, tarantella or the like?"
For castle-wide the worry'd spread:
Cole the Least, the first-born grandson
(destined for succession through a quirk
of primogeniture) had shown no sign
of readiness for ruling nor for barest
etiquette. The staff and servants wore
their shirts out making crosses
on their chests while asking God to send

some gravitas to younger Cole.

Too handsome by a half they said, and with
a predilection for the hunt but little
for his fellow man let alone the cunning
that his grandpa Cole the First had shown
before his brains unwound.

"It's time for him to take his draught," old Maude
announced as she surveyed the sundial
on the lawn. The Maude-invented draught
was one part mustard seed and one part
grated ginger root and two parts ale. It cleared his
sinuses and calmed his stomach and it helped him
to forget he had no memory.

He drank it from his chalice, belched and slid
down from his throne because he heard
the jolly fiddle tune. He grabbed a meaty hand
he hoped belonged to Maude (it did). Dancing needed
little brain because it lived inside the limbs, so
dance they did, while unbeknownst to all,
across the moat the duke of hoosiwhats
had sent a hundred hungry mounted men
with spears.

While she let herself be dipped and twirled,
Maude kept an eye upon the balcony,
another on the pulse in Cole's carotid arteries
(she feared his blood might reach a boil)
and the eyes they said she had behind her head,
those roamed the room. 'Twas large, the hall,
it sent an echo to the inner ears; she'd often said
she wished their kingdom wer'n't so small; she
wished that they could procreate a little faster
than they died, and then they'd fill this stony hall.

And all at once a plan took shape, a clever,
very risky one.

She motioned to her daughter Nell,
the one the most like her in sturdy build
and mien and grabbed Nell's hand
and placed it in her father's grasp;
Cole danced on, oblivious to queenly
subterfuge. In a trice Maude lifted
up her skirts and ran into the royal suite
and yanked the counterpane
clear off the bed, then yanked the canopy,
both darkest blue and velveteen. She flung
them o'er her shoulder then, and lifted up
her skirts once more and skittered down
the stony spiral steps and ran until
she found the shop below where servants
made the limey whitewash for the outer walls.
She caught her breath and spread
the counterpane upon the floor
and grabbed the widest brush in sight
and dipped it in and wrote in letters
two-foot high, an F, an R, a pair of Es,
as servants gaped at her, not knowing
how to read. Then she spread
the canopy and this time she wrote
WINE. Then down the hall to rouse
the kitchen maids and whisper questions
in their ears and issue frenzied orders
in response, then up the stairs with piles
of chalky velveteen to round up staff.
She brought them to the balcony
way high above the ground. Now get down
on all fours, she said. We're going to send
a sign. A scherzo played while she and they
walked on their hands and knees until

they reached the parapet. She stopped to catch
her breath and rub her scraped-up knees
and recall the better days when Cole
would send his rousing oratory out to all
the eager subjects of the realm.

Wine was rare for soldiers then,
and rarer still for peasantry.
Aware attack was imminent, Maude
showed the help how they should grasp
the velveteen across the top with all
their mustered might and then she whispered
"now" and they let the banners drop. Maude held
her breath and calculated sums: the mounted
hoosiwhatsit soldiers—how many mouths
had they? and hangers-on and passersby
would swell the ranks, but by how much?
The casks that lined the cellar wall—how many
tankards would they fill, and how many tankards
could the kitchen muster up? How many minutes
'til the message made its way from velveteen
into attackers' brains, and threw them off
their bloody path? She dared not peer
above the parapet so soon and risk an arrow
to the eyeball or projectile hurled by trebuchet.

Now stay right here and do not stand, she said,
and handed off her banner corner to the servant
next to her. Back inside, the dance was winding
down but Cole was going strong. Maude caught
the fish-eye from her daughter Nell, who clearly
wished to hand her father back. So Maude dismissed
her daughter with a kiss and danced once more
with Cole, quite pink and whiffy now.

The tuning fork inside Maude's brain—
it sensed a swelling of the castle ranks
before the other dancers noticed anything
amiss. And then commotion broke
like heaving waves into the hall,
with clanking boots of filthy soldiers
with their filthy hands a'gripping
every wine-fast vessel on the premises
and wine a'sloshing to the floor
and mouths a'cracking filthy jokes.
While Cole still held her tenderly
around the waist, Maude tilted up her head
toward God and prayed please send us
harmony, then placed two fingers
in her mouth and sent a curdling whistle
bouncing off the granite walls.

"Come join the dance," she called with all
her vocal strength, whereupon they heeded her
and Cole looked out with bulging eyes
and in the second just before his heart
gave way she felt his love—his love so rare,
none could compare.

Beside Her

I've nothing I can say in my defense.

That afternoon she sat upon
the stool I made her out of ash—
my sister Faye, a cunning thing with golden
ringlets and a twinkling laugh and a streak
of meanness that could raze a barn.

Earlier, Carmel the cook
had yelled the way she often did:
"come here right now me rascals
for I've poured ye each a bowl
of just-set farmer's cheese."

Instead of sitting next to Faye
and spooning up my curds and whey
I hid behind a bush nearby.

You should know that Faye
and I, we look alike, but only
on our surfaces. Our motivation
differs so: I am moved
to act by love and duty, while she
can't help defy. I often feel
my lip's been pierced
by many hooks attached
to fishing line that pull
me toward the house,
while she sticks out her
cunning little tongue at all
that goes on there.

My secret pet was large
and hairy as an old man's
ears. I found him on a rotten log

and lured him to an earthen jar
I fitted out with leaves and water
and when I thought about a name,
Iago is the first that came. I kept
Iago in a corner of the barn
where no one ever goes,
and I wound a length of twine
around the jar to make a cage
across the top from which Iago,
clever though he be, could not
escape, because he had so many
meaty legs and abdomen to match.
I fed him bugs I caught with tools I made
by sorting through the useful trash
Carmel left by the pantry door.

How odd it seems that girls
wear frocks and boys
do not. Earlier still that afternoon
the tutor shut his lesson book,
and Faye she fairly flew
into the freedom of the outdoor world.
I followed close behind as is my wont.

She called me Hughie,
which I barely tolerate,
and wagged her little tongue
at me and how I wished
she'd put it back inside. Then
she gathered up her frock
and ran away across the meadow
on her slippers made of
kid, daring me to find her
hidden in the brush.

"I know what we will do today!"

she said when found, her eyes
agleam. "We'll pretend
that I am you and you are me."
That's how I let her
talk me into trading
clothes. We stood apart
across the cover of a bush
and tossed our garments
overboard. I slipped
into her pale-blue frock
with smocking on the bodice
and I somehow sashed it up
in back. I felt as cool and free
as leaves blown by the breeze.
We closed our eyes and counted
up to ten and yelled
ta-da to heighten
the surprise of looking like
our other twin. How
my shirt and britches turned her
to a thuggish lad, her curls
all tucked inside my cap. And how
she belly laughed on seeing me
all flounced in blue. She handed
me the ribbon from her
hair. I tried to tie it to my fringe
to please her but I couldn't
gather up enough. I thought
perhaps that Nature'd made
an error and this was who
she'd meant for us to be.

Who knows why we are made
the way we are, protrusions here,
recesses there? Why she

is granted golden locks and I'm
expected to be shorn? Why she
for all her hardness fears the smallest
things that crawl, whilst I am tender
but adore the insect and arachnid world?

Come catch me, Hugh,
she said, and let herself
be caught and how I fought to hold
her fast inside my togs. She let me
play at victory, but then she slipped
right from my grasp and doubled back
and disappeared, leaving me to face
with naked knees and puffy sleeves
the wrath and snickers of the house.

It was then I hatched my scheme.

You see, they ordered me
to swap us back to proper
frock and britches. I also wore
a rising welt upon my nether cheek
inflicted by our father's belt.

My bowl of cheese sat by the kitchen
door while Faye plowed into hers,
unreprimanded and unharmed.

Behind my bush, unwinding all the twine
I whispered in Iago's face
but not too close; I'd asked the tutor
for a book of spider facts, but he
hadn't found one so I didn't know
yet if Iago was the sort to bite
his prey and if his bite
was venomous.

Iago seemed to understand my need
for he headed straight for Faye. How
beautiful and brilliant black he looked a-climbing
up her pale blue frock. I waited for some sound,
and when it came was like a thunder storm,
a thousand crows, the grist mill grinding wheat.

She wasn't bitten, no; I'd never wanted that.
But when she fled her slipper caught
upon a stone and tossed Iago to the wild
and tossed her toward a stone
that opened up her cheek. For once
I wasn't held to blame, for no one knew
my role. It matters little for I look ahead
and see her puckered cheek and know
there'll be a life of inward scars for me.

Just Another Jack

I don't believe they even named me
Jack, just called me by the syllable
that came most quickly to their lips;
they might as well have yelled "hey you,"
for Jacks were cheap—a fellow up the lane
who tumbled down a hill
and never was quite right again.
Another with digestive woes and one
who traded in his bony cow for beans.

And me? Who ever guessed
that I'd achieve a bit of local fame?
My mum passed on 'ere I was old
enough to hold the sight and smell
of her inside my brain. My dad?
A piece of wormy work who wiped his hands
of me and palmed me off on aunts
who croaked 'ere long: one kind
but in no sober shape to tend a boy,
the other sour as a lime.

I schooled myself, in chandlery.
A self-taught chandler's cottage
reeks of mutton fat, a chandler's skin and hair
both wear a coat of mutton fat.
A chandler's life is measured out
in accidents. That's not to say the danger's
on a scale of butchers who are often short
a thumb or two, but a chandler's apt
to have patch or two or three, sometimes
a field, of angry purple cross-hatched flesh
that's welded fast to bone.

But I had time and patience and I learned
to read whatever words I came across
upon a printed page. One time I found

a chemist's text and taught myself
to make a brew and glory in the sizzle
of an acid hitting base.

You can't imagine how enticing
was the competition at the time.
No one knew for sure what sparked
the vogue; some believed it warded
off the ague and yellow jack, others claimed
it harked to pagan rituals. But suddenly the lads
put down their darts and romanced fire.

Fire was my trade, and I was nimble
near a flame, and I was quick of mind. I sewed myself
a pair of leather britches, which required
two full fortnights: one to make a pattern
and another one to shove the needle
through the hide (I fin'lly forged an awl to ease
the needle's path and spare my finger pads).
Glad was I to have this task to fill the quiet nights.

The boniface knew well he had a goldmine
and he charged the crowd an entry fee
and ev'ry week he raised the platform up
a notch and ordered up an extra keg
to lubricate the crowd that came from burghs
an hour's wagon ride away to watch us lads be lads.
And every week the pool of winnings grew.

The tavern ceiling sagged so low that even ladies
sometimes snagged their hair. The walls were made
of wattle, daub and sand and dung. The air was close
with hand-hewn tables, benches, hordes whose bellies bulged
with drink, and fog of breath and barley-scented sweat.
The dartboard had been taken from its nail; instead
all eyes were on the wooden platform on which sat

the famous candlestick which leapt with every laugh
and belch and slam of door.

I went out to the trough and wetted down
my britches, secure that this would spare
my lower half from being set aflame if
(God forfend) I were to slip and fall.

Do not pitch your hopes too high, I told
myself, a lesson life had taught me well.
But while other jumpers flirted with the maid
who brought the ale and with the ale itself,
I read the flame. For after all, my trade
was tallow, suet, blubber, lard, smoke
and ember, cinder, ash. My boots were fleet,
my arms were quills that caught the current,
and my mind was clear in calculating arc
and clearance. My ears, the only part of me
to tipple, soon were drunk on cheering from
the mouths of those who never paid me any
mind before.

I won the pool for three weeks running
and became the one to beat and for the first
time ladies looked my way and overlooked
my scars. I took my silver home inside
my homespun pouch and the hound and I
we roasted proper meat and filled our bellies
for the first time ever.

Now, alas, the tavern's closed, the keeper
and his seven children ill (and he already
long a widower). For you see the fever
is again afoot, a devil that will turn
the whites of eyes to yolks then drench
the flesh in yellow too but not before

it causes a poor soul to vomit out
the greasy contents of his gut, not before
it sets an anvil on the head and daggers
in the spine and a mighty quaking fever
crown to toe. How cheap the rumors
of a treatment be—ipecac and castor oil
and enemas of turpentine to loosen up
what's jammed.

For a blessed spell I was a lucky lad.
Now as I've said the only schooling
I have had is that which I have taught myself—
a little bit from books, a lot from having time
to think and watch the world while using
common sense and here's one fact
I'll share with you whilst I can muster
strength to write a shaky hand: a candle flame
won't draw a fever out and fire can do much
but cannot cure disease. I pray for some good soul
to give the hound a home. If you call him
Jack he'll come.

Michele Herman is author of the novel *Save the Village* (Regal House Publishing, 2022) and the poetry chapbook *Victory Boulevard* (Finishing Line Press, 2018). Her poems, stories and essays have appeared widely in *The Sun, Ploughshares, The Hudson Review, The New York Times, Diagram, Lilith* and many other publications. She is a multiple Pushcart nominee, has been a semifinalist for the Raymond Carver Prize, and has won several writing awards, including two Willis Barnstone Translation Prizes and the Best Column Award from the New York Press Association. Her columns have run for many years in *The Villager* and more recently on the *The Village Sun* website. She teaches fiction, poetry and memoir at The Writers Studio, works as a freelance developmental editor and writing coach, translates French songs, and occasionally performs her own work in cabaret and theatrical settings. She is the mother of two grown sons and lives with her husband in Greenwich Village.

www.ingramcontent.com/pod-product-compliance
Lightning Source LLC
LaVergne TN
LVHW041507070426
835507LV00012B/1386